My Shoe

Mike Graf
Richard Morden

Rigby

www.Rigby.com
1-800-531-5015

Rigby Focus Forward

This Edition © 2009 Rigby, a Harcourt Education Imprint

Published in 2007 by Nelson Australia Pty Ltd ACN: 058 280 149
A Cengage Learning company

1 2 3 4 5 6 7 8 374 14 13 12 11 10 09 08 07
Printed and bound in China

Dirt on My Shoe
ISBN-13   978-1-4190-3805-1
ISBN-10   1-4190-3805-2

Dirt on My Shoe

Mike Graf
Richard Morden

Contents

Chapter 1

On the Trail

Jamil and Kaitlyn were hiking on the Rainbow Ravine Trail with their families.

As they walked along, Kaitlyn pointed to Jamil's feet. "Are you sure you want to take those brand new tennis shoes out here?" she asked.

Jamil laughed and said, "They're going to get dirty someday. Come on, let's go!"

Jamil and Kaitlyn took off running.

They raced to a small canyon.
There were colorful bands
of sandstone
along the trail.

Jamil and Kaitlyn turned a corner and stopped so they could catch their breath.
Kaitlyn realized that both their families were out of sight.

Chapter 2

The Canyon

Jamil and Kaitlyn climbed into
the dry, empty canyon.

They turned a corner
and looked up.
The steep cliffs were bright orange.
Large boulders jutted out
from the sides of the cliffs.

"Hello!" Jamil called out.

"Helloooo! Helloooo!" the canyon
echoed back.

"It's spooky here," Kaitlyn said.
"I wonder if anything has ever
lived here."

"I think so," Jamil answered.
"Millions of years ago,
places like this had lots of
plants and animals.
There might even be fossils here."

Jamil and Kaitlyn looked at
the ground.
They searched around for signs
of ancient life.

"Rocks, rocks, rocks,"
Jamil said,
turning over several stones.

"Not one fossilized bone,"
Kaitlyn said,
tossing a rock up the canyon.
"But look at your feet!"

Jamil looked at his new shoes.
They were covered in sand and dirt.
"Oh, well," he said.

Kaitlyn and Jamil climbed
a small hill above the trail.
They kept searching for fossils.

A few minutes later,
Jamil saw his dad looking up
at them.

"Hello up there," his dad shouted.

"It's time to come back!"
Kaitlyn's mom added.

Kaitlyn turned over one more rock.
"Nope. Nothing," she said.

Jamil grabbed a handful of dirt
and let it sift through his hand.
The dirt landed right on
his new shoes.

Dinosaurs

Kaitlyn and Jamil walked back
to the trail.

On the way back,
they passed a group of hikers.
A ranger was taking the group
on a guided hike.
The ranger stopped to talk
to the group just as Kaitlyn
and Jamil passed by.

"Millions of years ago,"
the ranger explained,
"there was lots of life up here.
But you would never know it now."

Jamil looked at Kaitlyn.
"See? That's what I told you!"
he said, smiling.

"In fact," the ranger continued,
"we have found fossils near here
of large and small dinosaurs."

Jamil and Kaitlyn stepped closer
to listen.

"Not all fossils are of animals,"
the ranger said.
"There are seashell and plant fossils
here, too.

"But fossils are usually hard to find. There are mounds of dirt to search. When most plants and animals die, they break down and become part of the soil."

"We should go, Jamil," Kaitlyn said.

Jamil nodded, and he and Kaitlyn ran to catch up with their families.

Chapter 4

The Paper Cup

"Hi there! You're back,"
said Kaitlyn's mom, smiling.

"Did you have a good look around?"
asked Jamil's dad.

"Yes, we did," Jamil answered.
"Why did we have to come back
so quickly?"

"Because we want to set up camp
before dark," Dad replied.

"We could have found a fossil though," Kaitlyn said.

"Maybe we can come back and join a paleontological dig," Jamil's dad suggested.

"I'd really like that," Jamil said.

Jamil and Kaitlyn waited to get
into the back seat of the car.
Kaitlyn opened the door.

"You're not going to get in there with all that dirt on your shoes, are you?" Kaitlyn asked Jamil.

Jamil looked at his new shoes.
They were filthy.
He could feel the dirt inside them.

Jamil thought for a minute,
then he grabbed a paper cup
from the back seat of the car.
Kaitlyn watched as he took off
his shoes and shook the dirt
out of both of them
into the paper cup.

"Now I'm ready to get in,"
Jamil said, smiling at Kaitlyn.

"What are you going to do
with all that dirt?" Kaitlyn asked.

"It's not just dirt," Jamil responded.
"I'm going to put it under
my microscope at home.
Maybe there are things in it
we can't see right now.
I can't wait to look!"